AMERICAN COUNTRY LIVING
KITCHENS
DECORATING, COOKING, AND ENTERTAINING

BARBARA RANDOLPH

CRESCENT BOOKS
New York

A FRIEDMAN GROUP BOOK

This 1992 edition published by Crescent Books,
distributed by Outlet Book Company, Inc.,
a Random House Company,
225 Park Avenue South,
New York, New York 10003.

ISBN 0-517-06115-5

AMERICAN COUNTRY LIVING:
KITCHENS
was prepared and produced by
Michael Friedman Publishing Group, Inc.
15 West 26th Street
New York, New York 10010

Editor: Robert Hernandez
Art Director: Jeff Batzli
Layout: Charles Donahue
Photography Researcher: Daniella Jo Nilva

Typeset by Bookworks Plus
Color separation by Scantrans Pte. Ltd.
Printed and bound in Hong Kong by Leefung-Asco Printers Ltd.

8 7 6 5 4 3 2 1

To all my country neighbors in whose kitchens I have spent many pleasant hours.

© Bill Rothschild/interior design by Lee Napolitano

CONTENTS

THE HEART OF THE COUNTRY HOME

A country kitchen begins with a frame of mind, not with a decorator's manual. By its very nature, a country kitchen is a comfortable place where family and friends gather to be a part of the household activity. A country kitchen is a busy place and its decor is born of the activities that are carried on there. It isn't a place where sticky fingers or messy projects are banned. Its sounds and scents are those of the foods that are created and shared there as well as the good times that naturally occur around its bountiful table.

Because a country kitchen isn't a decorator showpiece, it doesn't depend on a particular size or shape. Nor does it have to be in a home set deep in the woods or fields. A country kitchen, full of the aromas of fresh bread and pies in the oven, can be in a city apartment, the view from its windows a geometric skyline instead of the rounded green shapes of trees and distant hills.

While a large, roomy kitchen allows more space for bulky furnishings such as wood stoves, there is no one piece of furniture essential to a country kitchen. The wide farmhouse table can be replaced by a tiny breakfast table. Pick and choose those things from this book that will fit not only the space you have but your own style of living. Your country kitchen will not look or feel like anyone else's; it will be uniquely your own, and that is what makes it a real country kitchen.

Beams are perfect for displaying collectibles or storing useful, but bulky, cookware.

© Bill Rothschild/interior design by Jeanne Leonard

Country kitchens can combine the best elements of modern and traditional decor.

BEYOND EARLY AMERICAN

Although the "look" that we think of as country is often based on the antiques and implements of the past, a country style is not the property of any one place. It is instead the combination of many influences, blended together in an infinite number of ways. One of the beauties of a country kitchen is that anything goes. Here you can mix the simple lines of Shaker furniture with the froufrou of Victorian cast iron. Bright and busy tile patterns from Portugal can live in the same kitchen with Pennsylvania Dutch pierced-tin designs. Braided straw ornaments from Scandinavia or England are comfortable with terracotta pottery from Central America.

A WORLD OF COUNTRY STYLES

Just as American in its origins, although not reaching quite as far back into its history, the kitchens of the Southwest or Santa Fe style are among the most popular in country decorating. Like its Eastern counterparts, it relies on the traditional utensils and decorations of the area. Rich in terracotta tones and earth colors set against rough white stucco walls and highlighted with bright primary accents, this is a vital style.

The Southwestern kitchen is bright, airy, full of Native American motifs and lively Spanish decor. The colors spring from the deserts and skies: rich blues, sunset oranges, ocher, and russet sand shades. Pottery and baskets are used for containers, and a bright Navaho rug may cover the floor or a wall. Designs are solid and geometric, lines are clear, and the look is uncluttered.

Also born of a warm climate, where light and air are maximized in large open spaces, is the Mediterranean country kitchen. Primary colors predominate, set against creamy walls and dark wood tones. The furniture is rugged, and the work spaces are designed for a lot of use.

Bright designs are painted on tiles that may cover the walls, floors, or even countertops. Pottery is terracotta or painted, copper pots hang from hooks, and the ingredients themselves create decoration in the form of braided garlic cloves or bright purple onions. Like the Southwest, the cuisine and kitchen alike are enlivened by fiery bright red peppers hung in strings.

There are other variations. The French-Canadian country kitchen relies on time-worn implements, which are hung perhaps on a brick-fronted fireplace, but they are enlivened with bright pottery of Quimper or another whimsical design. The provincial touch is further provided in checkered linens and offset with plain white china. A Southern country kitchen welcomes the breeze with ruffled curtains of an almost gauzy white cotton, and a Midwestern farmhouse kitchen may add a freshly painted Hoosier cupboard to that look. In the northern Midwest, where the Scandinavian influence is strong, the cabinets may be painted in the bright, flowing designs of rosemaling.

The keynote of any country kitchen, whatever its particular style, is comfort, traditional designs, and the familiar warmth of home.

Tile countertops lend a Mediterranean flair to any kitchen.

© Monserrate Schwartz/FPG International

A working fireplace is both a focal point and a gathering place in a kitchen.

CHAPTER ONE

DECORATING IN COUNTRY STYLE

For the colonist of moderate means, the kitchen might well have comprised the whole house. But it was the first place to see "modernization." By the 1700s, conveniences such as the candle mold and roasting oven had made household chores less tedious, and the beds had moved from the kitchen to the bedrooms.

Prosperity brought China tea and porcelain cups to drink it from—at least when there was company. In the South, the kitchen of the more prosperous home was a separate building, used in the summer, to relieve the main living area from the added heat and danger of fire.

Later, the wood cookstove replaced the fireplace as a cooking place and source of heat, and it was better at both jobs. Slate or soapstone sinks replaced the washtub, and hot-water tanks attached to the wood stove replaced the ever-ready pot on the fire. Chairs replaced benches, and the table itself changed styles with the times.

By the early twentieth century, the black iron stove had become enameled in pale green or ivory, the pride of a housewife. Hoosier cupboards were painted to match. These minipantries had tin-lined bins for flour and sugar and a built-in flour sifter, as well as shelves for dishes, a pull-out work surface, and drawers for linens and bake ware. Today, these are among the most sought-after pieces of old kitchen furniture. They seem to represent American ingenuity, inventiveness, and the homely arts, all in one.

The pie safe, a cabinet with pierced tin doors and side panels that allowed air to circulate but kept flies off food, is another uniquely American piece of furniture. These were kitchen pieces, often painted and made of whatever wood was available, in whatever size struck the carpenter's fancy. They were often homemade, so their sizes, shapes, and styles vary enormously. (To replace tin panels, see tin piercing, page 45.)

The kitchen is probably the easiest room in your home in which to capture the wonderful country feeling. Homespun tablecloths and dish towels, crockery, wooden ware, glass canning jars, and baskets are all made in old styles and patterns. Old kitchen utensils are still available at flea markets and yard sales. Tin containers, cups, cookie cutters, and occasionally skimmers and apple corers are found, as well as gadgets from wooden-handled ice cream scoops to top-of-the-stove toasters.

Painted match safes from the 1940s blend with the nutmeg graters, wooden apple-butter paddles, stoneware crocks, and cast-iron waffle irons in a collection that can begin with whatever is available and grow in any direction. Some collectors specialize in one medium: tinware, cast iron, pottery, or wood. Others choose a specific purpose, such as nutmeg graters or implements and containers connected with herbs and spices.

Cookie cutters are still available and are fun to collect because of their varied shapes and designs. They are historically interesting as well, since it is easy to see their evolution and to spot those that were made of scrap tin by farmers. Aluminum ones from the 1930s and 1940s often had painted wooden handles, and modern ones represent current children's crazes, such as dinosaurs.

Old cookbooks are another useful collectible, and the recipes reflect the lifestyles of their time as well as the favorite foods. Along with the classics—original editions of *The Fannie Farmer Cookbook* and the handwritten "receipt books" full of homey tips—there are the advertisement cookbooks of the early twentieth century. These pamphlets came free with a product or could be ordered by sending a postcard or a box top.

© Al Michaud/FPG International

Antique shops such as this one in Norton, Georgia, are a good source of kitchen decorations.

Tin kitchen implements are still available at reasonable prices in antique shops and flea markets.

Baskets and old canning jars are favorite storage containers in the country kitchen.

© Hanson Carroll

Old implements can be displayed on a beam or hung under a shelf.

These small cookbooks are colorful, full of illustrations of smiling housewives in the day's popular hairstyles and pink-cheeked children reaching for another cookie. The recipes are the most innovative of their day, fresh from the test kitchens of Fleischmann's® Yeast, Baker's® Chocolate, Pillsbury® Flour, and other products. And they are so good that to this day these companies get requests for copies of a particular fudge or dinner roll that appeared in a booklet in the early part of this century.

Displaying these can be fun if you don't plan to use them, since they are colorful in small frames or grouped as a collage. Some collectors simply photocopy their favorite scone or cake recipe, then frame the original booklet.

Utensil collections can be hung from nails or hooks in a beam, or put in arrangements on the wall. Old mail-sorting cabinets make perfect display cases for these small items,

since they allow you to frame each piece or group separately and keep them all visible.

Some of the pieces can be used for storage or for their original purpose. Clown-shaped lemon squeezers from the 1920s still squeeze lemons, and a big tin breadbox is a fine place to store cereal boxes, crackers, or bread. Old cookie jars can be kept full of cookies (perhaps those from a turn-of-the-century flour recipe booklet), and crocks can hold wooden spoons and whisks within easy reach of the stove.

Old glass-topped canning jars or new replicas are perfect for storing dried beans, nuts, grains, and pastas. Lined up along narrow shelves under the upper cabinets or on an unused wall, these are decorative and save cupboard space. Baskets can hold fresh vegetables, pot holders, garlic, and small utensils; and round, wooden Shaker-style boxes stack easily and close snugly for shelf storage.

COUNTRY COLORS

Just as country decorating lends itself to many different styles—or to many combinations—nearly any color has its place here as well. While we think first of the warm rich tones of blue milk paint, dark red, old rose, and moss green, the bright primaries, russet earth tones, and pastels are all equally at home in a country kitchen.

There are no firm rules; your own eye will tell you how to mix and blend colors in a way you like. Comfort is the keynote.

Color is an inexpensive way to achieve a particular style—a coat of paint can change the mood or feeling in a room, even without making other renovations. Color is also a good way to tie together several different decorating styles. When planning colors, choose one to predominate and use it in 60 to 70 percent of your decorated areas (not counting the walls or floors, if these are plain wood, neutral white, or cream tones). That color might be used for wall or floor coverings or for a large piece of furniture. Then choose a secondary color that goes well with it, using it for curtains or other fabric coverings. A third accent color might be used to tie in small decorative items.

Your color scheme might be suggested by one major element used in the room, such as a rug, a chair or table, or curtains. You could choose two or three colors from it and repeat them elsewhere.

Rugs or other floor coverings are a good place to use your main colors together, since they provide a visual base for the room. Wallpapers can serve this same function.

Stenciling is a particularly good way to tie in different colors in a kitchen, since you can use whatever colors you like in your pattern. Stenciled walls can, for example, tie in the deep tones of painted wainscoting and door frames, pick up colors in the floor covering, or suggest new colors that could be echoed in table linens or towels.

The country kitchen need not be cluttered or filled with antiques to have a warm, homey feeling.

A wide window is the perfect place for a breakfast table.

© Melabee Miller/Envision

ADDING ARCHITECTURAL FEATURES

During all the recent public interest in preserving old architectural treasures, private interest has run just as strong. As owners make changes in their homes, they are on the lookout for clues to its past. Boarded-over fireplaces, heat registers, and covered tin ceilings are being rediscovered and restored.

But what of the buildings that never had these details or have lost them over the years? Fortunately, many of the old features can be added—retrofitted—or replaced. Tin ceilings, for example, can be purchased new and installed quite easily. Rough-hewn beams can be added to kitchen ceilings and studded with handwrought nails to look as if they'd been there for a century. Even decorative cast-iron floor registers can be installed.

© Bill Rothschild/interior design by Susan Honesty

© Robert Perron

Chair rails and other features can be added to give a new home the look of a previous century.

WALLS

The kitchen lends itself to simple wall treatments. While vinyl wallpapers are quite durable as well as washable, it isn't necessary to cover walls completely. Plain painted walls are the choice of many people for their country kitchens. Sometimes these are enlivened by a simple stenciled border.

One problem in choosing the wall covering for a kitchen is that the room tends to be a busy one in terms of its furnishings. The country-style kitchen is often decorated with the very implements that will be used (or have been in the past) there. As a background for displaying a collection of antique kitchen utensils, a plain painted or wood surface is much more attractive than a highly ornamented wallpaper pattern.

Wallpapers reproducing antique stencil designs do make good choices for a kitchen, especially if the colors are fairly pale. A simple stencil pattern that combines two light tones on a cream background is compatible with many kitchen decors and does not overwhelm other decorations.

Stenciling, done here by Leslie Powers, can add a decorative border or highlight panels in woodwork.

The kitchen table can be a working and social center of a country kitchen.

Painted or natural wood is another option. Dark wood wainscot panels or entire walls offer a good contrast to white appliances, keeping the kitchen from appearing all white while adding a note of warmth.

STENCILING WALLS

Stenciled borders have a timeless quality and an air of informal elegance that are particularly well suited to dressing up a kitchen. The best part about using stencils is that painting them requires absolutely no artistic talent.

Prepare the walls by painting them a neutral color (usually off-white). Choose a stencil design that fits the room and your decorating style—you can purchase ready-cut plastic film stencils in a wide variety of patterns. Brass stencils will last longer, but choose them only for larger designs without small patterns.

Acrylics are the best paints for stenciling walls. A jar holding less than one-eighth of a cup of paint can decorate a whole kitchen, and you are almost sure to have some left over for other stencils.

Use stiff stencil brushes, one for each color. Put a little acrylic paint onto a piece of glass and lightly dip the brush into it. On a folded paper towel, wipe most of the paint from the brush until it appears almost dry. Lay the stencil on a piece of heavy paper and paint over the openings of the stencil using an up-and-down, circular scrubbing motion to push the bristles onto the surface of the paper. Keep the brush dry—the least smear under the stencil means you are using too much paint. Go over an area several times to darken the color, but don't use more paint.

If you are stenciling a room with many doors or windows, plan your "repeat" so you don't leave off halfway through a design. Designs without a formal repeat are easier to space, as are motifs that are repeated often in a short space. You can make light pencil marks on the wall to guide your stencil placement. When you are ready to paint, attach the stencil to the wall with masking tape.

For chair rails, a yardstick will give you the right height, and you can make a straight edge to follow by using a chalk

Stenciled designs around windows can cheerfully decorate even an ordinary home.

line (a string rubbed in colored chalk and snapped against the wall to leave a line).

Clean the stencils frequently with warm water. Nail-polish remover scrubbed on with an old toothbrush will remove paint buildup on brass stencils. It is important to clean stencils often to keep paint from filling in the holes and making your design shrink as you work around a room.

Always clean stencils on a flat surface. Be sure to clean the brushes well with soap and warm water before storing them away.

Your stenciled design does not need to be covered with a fixative. Wash stenciled walls just as you would wash any painted wall, taking care not to scrub or use harsh abrasives or scouring powders.

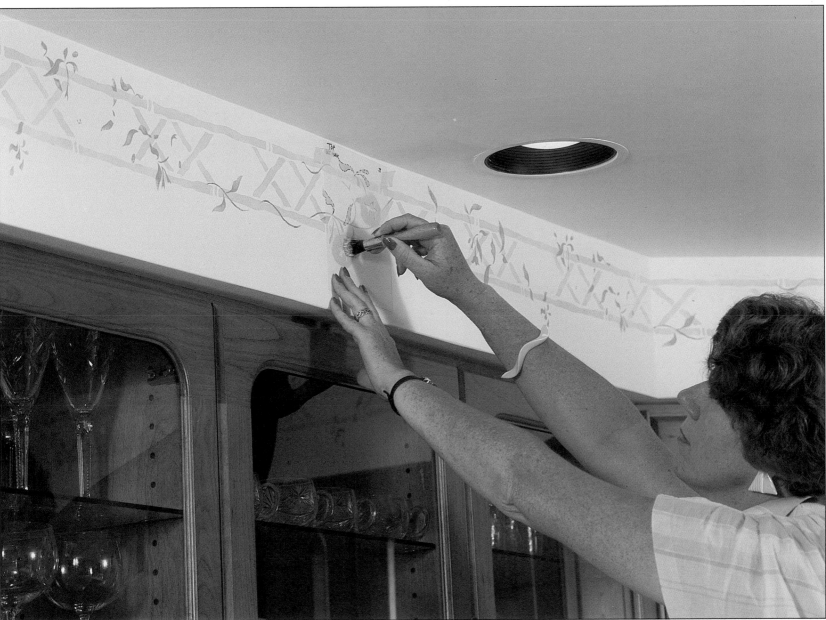

Leslie Powers demonstrates the proper use of a stencil brush.

Decorative borders highlight cabinet work.

DECORATIVE MOLDINGS

Even new kitchens can be given early American features with the creative use of inexpensive, precut molding strips from a lumber store. Chair rails, window cornice boards, boxed beams, and rich antique door frames can be put in place over a weekend.

These details add the finishing touch to an otherwise undistinguished kitchen, and when painted an antique color and combined with historic wallpapers and drapery fabrics, they can transform the entire room.

First, take careful stock of the room and be sure of how you want to dress it up. A very informal, small kitchen might look strange with elegant window and door-frame moldings, but a combined dining room and kitchen might be just the place for this touch of a fine old home. Consider

A border of decorative molding highlights a set of shallow shelves.

© Robert Perron

If a kitchen does not have real beams to expose, these can be added below the existing ceiling.

how wainscoting will visually alter the dimensions of the room. By cutting it in half crosswise, it will make the ceiling seem lower and the walls seem longer. If all the furniture in a room is table-height with no mantel or cabinet piece to give a vertical line, chair rails can also make the room seem cut in half.

To add chair rails, you will need only a simple narrow piece of molding to finish off the edge underneath a 1-inch-wide strip of plain board set at chair-back height. To border windows or door frames, you will want a fairly plain molding that's narrow enough so it won't stick out beyond the thickness of the frame boards.

To add a ceiling cornice, you can use either a wide strip of molding or you can make elegant ones for high-ceilinged rooms by placing a 2-inch strip of board along the upper wall next to the ceiling. Add two strips of molding: one against the ceiling and a narrower one along the wall below the board.

Cover these molding strips with primer before putting them in place. Use finishing nails, which should be set below the surface of the wood. Fill in the holes with wood putty before painting the molding to match the rest of the woodwork in the room.

Raised paneling can be created by using panels of wide boards and surrounding them with molding. These are particularly attractive on a wall above a mantel.

Instead of the more formal look of painted moldings and paneling, you may choose to use a chair rail of natural wood to finish off wainscoting of unpainted pine or cherry. Since new pine is often a very light color, you may wish to tone it down by rubbing it with a cherry or walnut stain.

BEAMS AND RAFTERS

What would a country kitchen be without beams for hanging baskets, herbs, old tinware, and cast-iron pans? The beauty of these is that you can change the decorations to correspond with the seasons. Hang flowers to dry in the fall, herbs in the winter, and canning ladles and garden baskets in the summer. At Christmas, wrap beams in balsam roping or hang spicy pomanders there to dry.

If you haven't found any old square nails in your house, you can buy them at hardware stores. Blacksmiths will make you beautiful iron hooks with sharp ends that you can pound right into the beams.

While old beams aren't just lying around for the taking, they are available from salvage companies or from old barns and outbuildings that have been torn down. (In rural areas, it is sometimes possible to buy these directly from owners of fallen-in sheds.)

New beams can be purchased from lumber suppliers, but even with a coat of dark stain, they do not have the rough-hewn and weathered look of old wood.

Beams can unify a kitchen by tying together dissimilar elements and drawing in large spaces.

Baskets and dried flowers can decorate a beam, while remaining within handy reach.

All the comforts of this country kitchen make it an inviting room to work in.

LINENS AND CURTAINS

Because of the natural informality of a country kitchen, there is a wide range of possibilities for the treatment of windows. Many people choose to let in all the light available and have no curtains at all in the kitchen. Another way to accomplish this is to have only a top ruffle or cornice curtain and narrow side curtains. These frame the window without cutting out light or a view.

Curtains of thin white fabric allow maximum light, and cut a not-so-country view. These also have the advantage of being easily washable, a necessity for any fabric used in an active kitchen. Unbleached muslin is a good fabric choice for a kitchen, combining washability with a homespun, informal appearance. Muslin also takes well to stenciling, with its slightly off-white surface, and can be used for table linens as well as curtains.

Silky damasks and other formal decorative fabrics are not generally suitable for the country kitchen, but there are some very attractive cotton "homespun" fabrics, especially in blue or old reds. These bring a distinctive aura of the past to a kitchen when used either as curtains or as tablecloths and napkins.

There is no rule that a kitchen table must have a tablecloth. In fact, if the table is used as a work area, a tablecloth may be a real nuisance. Bare wood lends warmth, and even at dinner it need not be covered.

STENCILING TABLECLOTHS AND NAPKINS

Measure your table and add at least 18 inches of overhang on each side. Unless the table is very small, the resulting figure will be more than the normal 45-inch width of unbleached muslin. Since a single seam up the center of the tablecloth isn't attractive, you should make the tablecloth in four panels, joined by a crossed seam at the center.

To do this, begin with the measurements of the finished tablecloth as determined above. Divide each dimension by two, so that you have the measurement of one-fourth of the

Table linens add a touch of elegance to a meal served in the kitchen.

Brightly colored linens can add warmth and life to a light-colored kitchen.

tablecloth. For example, if your table is 30 by 40 inches, you would add 36 inches to each dimension (18 times 2), giving you 66 by 76 inches for your finished tablecloth. Each of the four sections would then be 33 by 38 inches.

Cut the prewashed muslin to make four pieces this size. Using a half-inch seam, stitch these four pieces together into a rectangle. Press the seams of the first two sections open before you stitch the two halves together, so that you will have a perfectly flat seam. Be sure your seams are straight—any curve will show up as a lump in the tablecloth. It's a bit tedious, but you will have better luck if you baste the pieces together first.

Press all the seams flat and topstitch just the width of your sewing machine foot away from the seam (this makes it quite easy to keep the stitching straight). The topstitching will hold the rough edges flat and give a finished look to the seams. Be sure the thread matches the fabric perfectly. Hem the outer edges with a narrow hem and iron the tablecloth.

Choose a fairly simple stencil pattern with no more than three colors. The design can be a relatively large one, which you will stencil only in the four corners where the panels meet in the center and at the four outside corners. Or you could choose a border design that you stencil along

Tile countertops and old crockery give a provincial flair to a modern kitchen.

each seam and the hem, just inside the stitching. This will give you a finished pattern of a border and a double row forming a cross at the center of the table.

You will need one stencil brush for each color. Brushes to be used for the large openings of the stencil should be fairly big and those that will be used in smaller spaces should be smaller. All should be the short, stubby brushes designed especially for stenciling. Use acrylic stencil paints intended for use on fabric. These come in very tiny jars, and you will need only one jar of each color. Since you use very little paint, it goes a long way.

Pad your work surface with several sheets of newspaper and cover it with a clean piece of fabric. (An old worn-out sheet works well, but a dish towel will do.)

Cut a scrap of the muslin or a similar fabric to use as a practice piece. Lay the stencil over the fabric and secure at the corners with masking tape.

Put a little smear of paint on a piece of glass or on the bottom of an old plate. Dip the brush into it just enough to pick up a tiny spot of paint. Rub the brush on a folded paper towel to remove most of the paint. All you want left is the color—there should be no paint on the brush.

Using short stabbing motions with the brush, rub the color into the fabric through the openings in the stencil. Do not rub back and forth or you will pull the fabric and change its position under the stencil. To make the color darker, keep working in the color with the brush. Add new paint only when you cannot get any more color from the brush. Be sure to rub the excess paint onto the paper towel before you apply the brush to the fabric each time.

When you have perfected the technique and can make a perfect design with clean edges, you are ready to stencil the tablecloth. Be sure to measure the placement of the designs carefully before you begin. You can mark these with tailor's pencils, which will come out of the fabric easily.

When the entire tablecloth is completed, iron the designs from the reverse side, using a warm iron. This will help to set the colors.

Cut the napkins and either hem or fringe the edges by raveling out the threads along each edge to a quarter-inch width. If the design you use on the tablecloth is a large one, you can repeat it in miniature or simply choose a single element from it to repeat on the napkins. If you choose a border, you can either repeat one element or, if it is a small design, you can stencil it all around the edge of the napkin as you did along the hem of the tablecloth.

Acrylic paints, brushes, and stencils are all you need to design your own personalized tablecloths and napkins.

FLOORS

There are a number of attractive, practical ways to cover kitchen floors. Plain floorboards need no coverings or may be accented with runners or small throw rugs. These should have a firm surface, such as hooked or braided, if they are to be used in heavy-wear areas. They are less suitable for floors directly in front of the sink and stove, where they are more likely to become stained. Woven grass mats or rugs can be used in living areas of the kitchen, but are not sturdy enough for a cooking area.

Stenciled floor cloths have come back after a century of oblivion, and are especially well suited to kitchens. Easy to make and keep clean, they can cover an entire floor or protect a much-used area with a warm accent.

Commercial floor coverings come in a variety of styles, replicating Mediterranean country tiles, stones, brick, and other surfaces. These are easy to care for in work areas of kitchens. Real tile is good for entry areas and under wood stoves, where it is the safest floor covering. In warmer climates, tile can be used for the entire kitchen floor, but tends to be a cold surface to stand on in places with cold winters. Brick is too rough for kitchen floor areas, except for hearths, entries, and under wood stoves.

BUILDING A WIDE-BOARD FLOOR

One of the most basic early American features, especially in a country home, is wide pine floorboards. But, sadly, the homeowner can't just rip up existing floorboards and lay an old wide set in their place. The main reason is that wide boards are not usually available, and when they are, they are usually so full of knots that they are unsuitable for floors.

The best place to look for wide boards is not at your local lumber store but at small lumberyards that treat each tree separately. These yards distinguish the big trees with fewer lower limbs and cut them separately.

Polished wood floors and natural wood furniture surfaces add warmth to a kitchen.

Be sure that the boards have dried for at least four to five months and have them planed on one side only. It is the planing that makes a board you buy as 1-inch stock actually only three-quarters of an inch thick. By having the rough-cut board planed on only one side, you will have a seven-eighth-inch thickness, which cuts down on warping.

At this point, you must have at least the patience of Job, because the boards need to dry and season for a year. They should be kept indoors in a heated area, stacked with space between the layers and each board. A purist will turn the stack over about halfway through the year, changing the order and direction of each board. Pine boards shrink a lot for a long time, so you want them to be as close to their final size as possible before you put them down.

Consider the visual effect of the direction of your floorboards. Lay them crosswise in a long, narrow room to prevent it from looking like a bowling alley. If the house is old and the floor joists uneven, you may have an occasional mound after you lay the subflooring. If this is the case, you will have to lay floorboards in the same direction as the lumps, not across them. Otherwise, the floor will bounce and board ends will pop up and become uneven after a while.

After seasoning, the widths of the boards will vary slightly, which makes it difficult to match them up end to end. If all the boards are the same length, begin each row from alternate sides of the room, so all the boards don't end in the same place, creating one long line running the width of the floor.

If you still have any patience left, leave the boards in place after you have laid them, but don't nail them down. You want the wood to continue to shrink and move, and you want it to acquire a little character and a few scratches before you put a finish on it.

After a few months (but not in the summer if you live in a humid climate), tap the boards to close the spaces and fill in with more as needed. Nail the boards in place, keeping the nails at least 1 inch from the edges and 2 inches from the ends. Go back over them with a tool called a nail set to sink the heads slightly below the surface.

A well-sealed, false-grained floor finish will withstand wear in low-traffic areas.

Sand the floor very lightly, just to even the edges and remove any rough places the planing missed. Vacuum and wipe the floor with a tack cloth to pick up all the sawdust.

Seal the floor with several coats of good finish, sanding between coats. Be very careful when choosing a stain, since nearly any one labeled "pine" will have a bright yellow tint that doesn't improve with age. Protect the finished floor with wax and clean it with Murphy's oil soap and warm water. Soon your floor will develop its own patina of age—and a few cracks between its boards. The vision of how wide those cracks would have been had you not let the boards season well will be the reward for your patience.

A wood floor, unbroken by rugs, adds a sense of space to a kitchen.

PAINTED FLOOR CLOTHS

Painted canvas floor cloths were among the earliest American floor coverings, both protecting the soft pine floors and adding a layer of insulation underfoot. Because of their age (they were most common in the 1700s) and heavy use, very few survive to tell us what designs were used. But early descriptions and the few remaining examples suggest that designs were often geometric or "faux" finishes made to look like marble or granite. Since floor cloths were meant to be walked on, the colors were probably dark and the designs simple.

In a modern setting, any one of several styles and designs is appropriate. The pattern you choose can be enlarged or replaced with another stenciled design. Or geometric designs can be created with masking tape.

You will need the heaviest canvas available, cut 2 inches larger each way than the dimension you wish for your finished floor cloth. You will also need a good-quality yardstick, gesso compound, fine sandpaper, Sobo® glue, a 3-inch nylon brush, a 3-inch varnish brush, satin finish interior polyethylene, paint thinner, masking tape, sharp pencils, eraser, a stencil (or stencil paper and knife), a stencil brush, acrylic stencil paints, and enamel interior paint for a base color.

Using the masking tape, cover 1 inch of the outside edge of the canvas all around. Keep the inner-edge line straight, since this will form the edge of the finished cloth.

Mix one-half cup each of the gesso, water, and Sobo® glue, and apply with the nylon brush first to one side, and then, when it is dry, to the other. When both sides are thoroughly dry, apply two coats of interior paint, to one side only, in the color that you have chosen for the base. Let the paint dry thoroughly between coats, and sand very lightly if the surface appears to be rough after the first coat. When the cloth is thoroughly dry, you are ready to stencil.

To cut the stencil, trace the design on stencil paper and very carefully cut along the outline, using an X-acto knife and cutting against a sheet of glass. Keep the edges perfectly smooth.

Stenciling is the most common decoration for painted floor cloths.

© Robert Perron

Using a yardstick, mark off the arrangement of the stencil design on the rug with a pencil, allowing for even borders.

Tape the stencil firmly in place. Touch the tip of the brush to the stencil paint and brush off the excess on a paper towel. The brush should be dry enough that only a little color comes off, but if you are using a dark color over a lighter one, you may have to use a little more paint. It is better to go over the opening several times than to risk having paint run under the stencil. If this should happen, remove the stencil and wipe the cloth and stencil quickly with a wet paper towel to remove the paint. Let both dry and begin again. In case of an error that cannot be cleaned off, you can repaint that portion of the rug to cover it.

When the stenciling is completed, allow the cloth to dry overnight, then apply three coats of polyethylene, drying overnight between each coat. Remove the masking tape and glue back the cut edges, trimming the corners diagonally to make square angles. When the glue is dry, give the entire cloth another coat of polyethylene.

Your floor cloth is both durable and washable and can be used in heavy-traffic areas, such as in front of the kitchen sink and under the table. It can be washed with hot water and detergent. If the surface should begin to wear, another coat or two of polyethylene will restore it.

Designs for hooked rugs can be as fanciful as your imagination suggests.

MAKING A HOOKED RUG

There is considerable discussion over whether the early hooked rugs were made of yarn or strips of wool fabric, but for today's craftsman, wool flannel fabric gives the most durable and attractive results and is easier to work with. The finished rug is smooth, tight, and long-lasting.

While it is possible to hand-cut one-eighth-inch strips of wool fabric, it is also a difficult and enormous job to do for an entire rug. There is a small, hand-cranked machine that does this quite easily (it looks like the fettucine blade on a pasta machine), or precut strips may be purchased. The latter is sometimes the most economical if only a few strips of a color are needed for shading, but the cutting machine is a good investment if you are doing even a small rug.

Along with the cut strips, you will need a backing of good-quality burlap—about 8 inches larger each way than the final rug will be—a hook (which can be purchased at needlework shops), and a rug frame. If you do not have a frame, you can make a simple one of four sturdy strips of wood secured into a rectangle. An old picture frame will work if it is sturdy. Attach the burlap to this frame with pushpins.

Before attaching the burlap, it should have a pattern on it. Rug-supply houses sell these already printed, or you can draw your own. Designs of old rugs were often quite primitive, so don't worry too much about your artistic talent.

Patterns of squares or rectangles were common, sometimes with a flower or fruit design in each square, or sometimes alternating. These small designs are especially easy to draw. Measure the squares onto the burlap, marking along a yardstick with a soft lead pencil. Tack the burlap to a sheet of plywood or other surface to hold it even as you draw. The designs in each square can be drawn freehand or transferred with carbon.

The colors are your own choice. Checkerboard rugs often alternated black squares with gray-toned ones, with the designs in the gray squares. You could choose a solid color that suits your room, and bring out a secondary color in the flowers or fruit. When working the designs in each square, do the motifs first, then fill in the background.

To make the rug, hold the hook in the right hand and the strip of wool in the left. (Reverse this if you are left-handed.) The wool is used in pieces about a foot long, and is held underneath the pattern. Push the hook between the threads of the burlap with the smooth side going between the thumb and first finger of your left hand and the hooked side touching your thumb. It should slide under the strip of wool and catch it as you draw it up through the burlap again. A slight pressure on the smooth side as you bring it up will open the threads slightly and allow the hook to pass through easily.

When you begin, the end of the wool strip should be brought to the top and about three-quarters of an inch left loose (it will be trimmed later). Push the hook into the next space between the threads and bring up a loop about an eighth of an inch high. Repeat this step, going into the next space each time, unless the loops become too tightly packed, in which case skip one occasionally to make them lie evenly. The loops should touch each other but not be so tight as to pucker the burlap. When you come to the end of the strip of wool, bring it through and trim both ends to the height of the loops.

Medallion designs were especially popular in the late nineteenth century, usually with floral patterns in each section.

If the previous loop slips when you pull up the next one, twist the hook away from you as you pull it through. With very little practice, you will find that the loops are of even height and the work smooth. If at any point you are not satisfied with a set of loops, you can simply pull out that strip and work it again.

When the rug is completely hooked, iron the entire rug from the back using the steam setting. On the sewing ma-chine, zigzag stitch around the outside of the hooked area, about three-quarters of an inch away from the edge, or make two rows of straight stitching side by side. Cut off one-quarter-inch of excess burlap outside the stitching. Stitch rug tape to the burlap (don't use iron-on tape, since it tends to pucker the edges) and hand-hem the other edge of the tape to the back of the rug. Be sure to miter the cor-ners by clipping them so they won't be too bulky.

Folk-art designs, with their bold colors and simple lines, adapt well to the technique of rug hooking.

TIN PIERCING

Tin piercing, like most other folk arts peculiar to America, was born of necessity. Although it is now enjoyed as a decorative feature, in the past the beautiful designs of old pierced tin simply added an aesthetic note to the panels that were the forerunner of modern screening.

Pies and other baked goods attracted flies, so pie safes, or pie cupboards, were made with pierced holes that let air flow through, but kept bugs out. Lanterns were also made of pierced tin, which let the candlelight out while protecting the flame from breezes.

Since the purpose of the old panels was to let as much air through as possible, there were a lot of holes. Geometric designs worked well, with diamonds, stars, sunbursts, and, especially in Pennsylvania, hearts and tulips. We can use the pierced lines to carry out design themes in other decorative items, such as wallpaper or stencil designs.

Tinsmiths use a tool called a bar folder to turn neat edges on tin, thus strengthening them and eliminating sharp edges. This isn't exactly a common piece of household equipment, so modern home craftsmen will probably want to frame pierced-tin panels for display, unless, of course, they are making them for use in a pie safe or to decorate the doors of kitchen cupboards. The easiest way is to choose the frame, then cut the tin to fit.

Trace the pattern on a piece of plain paper the size of the tin panel. Tape it in place over the panel. Do the piercing work on an old board, a piece of Sheetrock, or pad the work surface with at least a half-inch of newspaper. Use a sharp-pointed nail or an ice pick as the piercing tool.

Place the tool on the first dot and strike it gently with a hammer or a small wooden mallet. You will need to strike hard enough to pierce the tin with the point of the tool, but not so hard as to drive the entire shaft through it. With a little practice you will know how hard to strike in order to make uniform holes. When the design is complete, remove the pattern. You can rub the surface of the tin with olive or vegetable oil to protect it from rust if you desire, but do so carefully, because the holes are like a grater.

This pierced-tin panel is augmented with a hand-painted, geometric design.

© Robert Perron/Isaac Maxwell metalwork

Although pierced tin was originally used in pie safes, it can be adapted to nearly any paneled furniture or cabinet.

If you wish to make an unframed panel, you can fold back the cut edge by hammering it with a wooden mallet along the side of a straight edge. Handle it very lightly, since it will not be as smooth as one done on a bar folder, but if done carefully the edges will look fine and will be a lot safer. Measure the panel 1 inch longer and wider than you wish the finished piece to be. Mark the panel a half-inch from each edge of the corner and draw a diagonal line. Cut off the corners along this line.

Place the panel on a board with a sharp square edge and hold securely in place with one edge of the tin extending a half-inch over the edge of the board. With a wooden mal-let, gently tap the extended tin to bend it down. When you have formed a clean right angle, turn the tin over so the edge extends upward and tap it gently down against the tin sheet. Repeat with all the other edges. You can make holes for hanging just below the turned edge along the top. Be sure they are evenly spaced from the sides so it will hang straight.

If you wish to create a design using straight lines instead of dots, use a sharp chisel. Be careful to keep these straight chisel punches parallel, not running in a line, since they weaken the tin and will cause it to break apart along the indentations.

Antique shops in the South or Atlantic states, such as this one in Maryland, are more likely to have original tin pie safes.

CHAPTER TWO

DISPLAYING KITCHEN COLLECTIONS

By their very nature, old kitchen utensils are at home hanging from kitchen rafters, stacked in corners, or arranged in display cabinets made from old store crates. They were made to be used in the kitchen and still belong there.

Hutches, spice chests, pie safes, quilt racks, thread cabinets, iceboxes, type trays, store crates, Shaker boxes, baskets, coatracks, and silverware trays are all good containers for collections as well as being collectibles themselves.

Stack crates or boxes to create an irregular set of shelves. Hang shallow ones on the wall as shelves. Type trays make shadow-box shelves for miniatures or a mixture of small objects. Quilt racks make perfect towel racks and are good for displaying linens.

Use old cubbyhole mail cabinets to display a collection of small kitchen utensils. Since many kitchen pieces were designed to hang, these look nice on handwrought nails or hooks against a wooden or plaster wall or along the end of a kitchen cabinet. A beam is a good place to hang larger utensils, baskets, cast iron, or graniteware.

Many country collectibles are containers that can be used for their original purpose and decorate your kitchen at the same time. Use old tins for storing dry ingredients in the kitchen or pantry, baskets to hold rolled kitchen towels, and wooden boxes to store cleaning supplies. Arrange boxes and baskets on open shelves as decorative containers.

© Mark E. Gibson

COLLECTING KITCHEN ANTIQUES

Assembling an assortment of old or unusual kitchen gadgets makes browsing in antiques shops, flea markets, and yard sales a real treasure hunt. Collecting can mean looking for things that are different in nature and use, or concentrating on items for a particular purpose or those from a certain era in history.

Instead of looking for just any kitchen utensil, consider collecting graters, or narrow the field even further and collect only old nutmeg graters. Search for obsolete kitchen implements such as a cork-sizer or a meat juice-extractor or cream separator. Try to find as many kinds of food choppers as possible. Since these were common, everyday items, there are still plenty of them to be found in flea markets and antique shops.

WHERE THE TREASURES ARE

In your search for kitchen collectibles, be sure to tell your friends about your interest, and ask them to look in their attics and sheds. Other than the barn your grandmother stored things away in, there are several good sources of furniture and utensils.

ANTIQUES SHOPS vary greatly, but are usually the most expensive sources. Look for shops away from heavily traveled routes and tourist destinations, and remember the price range of the items you are interested in as you see them in various shops.

ANTIQUES SHOWS are gatherings of dealers that set up and display their pieces in one place for a day or a weekend. You will find a wide variety of small items at these shows and will have a chance to compare prices easily. Although most dealers bring smaller pieces and collectibles to shows, you may also find some furniture and larger items. A good tip for antiques shoppers is that early morn-

ing is the best time for rare items; late afternoon is best for bargaining.

ANTIQUES MALLS are permanent antiques shows where a number of dealers have space under one roof. Some malls have separate shops where each dealer sells his own merchandise, while others work on a cooperative basis with many displays and a central checkout. There is not much chance of discussing the prices in the latter type, but you should ask, since some use codes to show the lowest price they will accept.

AUCTIONS are excellent places to find country antiques, if you can resist the excitement that sometimes takes over during fast bidding. Best are house auctions, right on location, since they often bring out boxes full of unsorted treasures late in the day. Here's where you will be most likely to find the kitchen gadgets. If you are looking for rarer pieces or furniture, try to go early so you can look things over carefully and decide your top bid before the auction begins.

FLEA MARKETS are less formal than antiques shows, and often are held out of doors. A lot of secondhand and new items are mixed in, making it a real challenge to find the treasures. But if you go early, you can find some bargains, especially in kitchen utensils of the 1930s and 1940s.

YARD SALES can yield some very good finds and unbeatable prices, but you have to get to these before the antiques dealers do. You also may have to look for a long time, but you can find some surprising gems at prices that reflect a house-cleaning mood.

You never know where you will find the perfect addition to your kitchen collection—yard sales, junk shops, or a fine antiques market.

HOW TO SHOP

Most flea markets, yard sales, and antiques shops are good places to ask for a better price. Larger or metropolitan galleries may have fixed prices, but most others are flexible. How you inquire about price policies depends on your own attitude toward bargaining. Usually the simple question, "Is this the best price you can give me on this?" will tell you whether there is any room for negotiation.

A less direct way is to indicate your interest in something, but hesitate and move on to look at other items. A dealer who sees you returning several times to look at the same item and is willing to bargain will usually suggest a better price at some point.

Poke about to see what's there before asking for a particular item. If you enter a shop or booth and immediately ask for ice cream scoops, you are placing yourself at a disadvantage in bargaining. But before you leave a shop, it is wise to ask, since the owner may have pieces that are not on display.

At markets where items are jumbled together, try to picture the individual piece as it would look alone.

Even city antique shops, such as this one in Trenton, New Jersey, are likely to have pieces for your kitchen.

SHOPPING FOR CRAFTS

The decorations and furnishings for a country home need not be antiques. The charm of the country style is that it is the perfect showcase for handcrafted or one-of-a-kind pieces, old or new. There are several good sources for fine handicrafts.

ARTISAN'S COOPERATIVES are run by art associations or groups of craftsmen, and offer a wide selection of crafts, often at lower prices than gift shops. The advantage, too, is that everything you find in these places is handmade, where gift shops tend to mix handwork with mass-produced items.

CRAFTSMEN'S STUDIOS are usually the best place to shop for larger items and those that need to be made on special order, such as wrought-iron utensils or handmade rugs. You can watch the craftsman work, see samples in progress, and discuss your special needs. Nothing beats dealing directly with the craftsman. But studios are often widely separated and off the beaten path. When you are traveling, ask the local tourist office for a map or listing of craftsmen's studios in the area. Many publish these and you can quickly check to see if there are any that interest you along your route.

CRAFT SHOWS are the next best way to meet the craftsmen and see their work. These vary greatly in size, quality, and style, so you are best to choose a large, well-established show or one that is run by an artists' or craftsmen's organization or art council.

IMPORT SHOPS usually have beautiful handmade items for sale, and some of these have just the right touch for the country kitchen. Terracotta and painted pottery, tiles, woodenware, tin lighting fixtures, brightly painted bowls, baskets, and a variety of informal and lively decorative items abound in these shops.

Brick is the perfect background for displaying brightly polished copper pieces.

COLLECTING OLD NAPKIN RINGS

Silver (and later silver-plate) napkin rings offer a glimpse into the lives of generations past. Since many were engraved with at least a first name, there is a personal touch to each one. They are enormously varied in style, size, and decoration, but they can be mixed on a table without looking untidy.

Some are finely patterned in baroque designs, light both in weight and style. Some have pierced scroll shapes on their surface. Others are wide and heavy, with designs and beaded edges. They are frequently engraved: Zebediah, Sarah, Abigail, and other old-fashioned names appear. Often there is a date and an additional inscription to identify it as a presentation piece: "To Hattie, from her boarders," or "Sophronia, born August 2, 1883." Some have only initials.

In the late Victorian era, silver plate became popular as napkin rings became larger, heavier, and more ornate. The figural rings became popular—birds and animals posed against plain rings, or a ring and a baby chick both attached to a wishbone. Many people collect only figural rings.

Silver and metals were not the only materials used for napkin rings. Wood was popular, and wooden rings with black etchings of hotels, landmarks, and vacation spots became favorite souvenirs for traveling Victorians. Niagara Falls, lighthouses, and scenes in the Catskills and White Mountains all show up on these wooden rings. They were inexpensive gifts to bring home at the time, and today are still less expensive than silver antiques.

This elegant table setting is enhanced by the antique napkin rings.

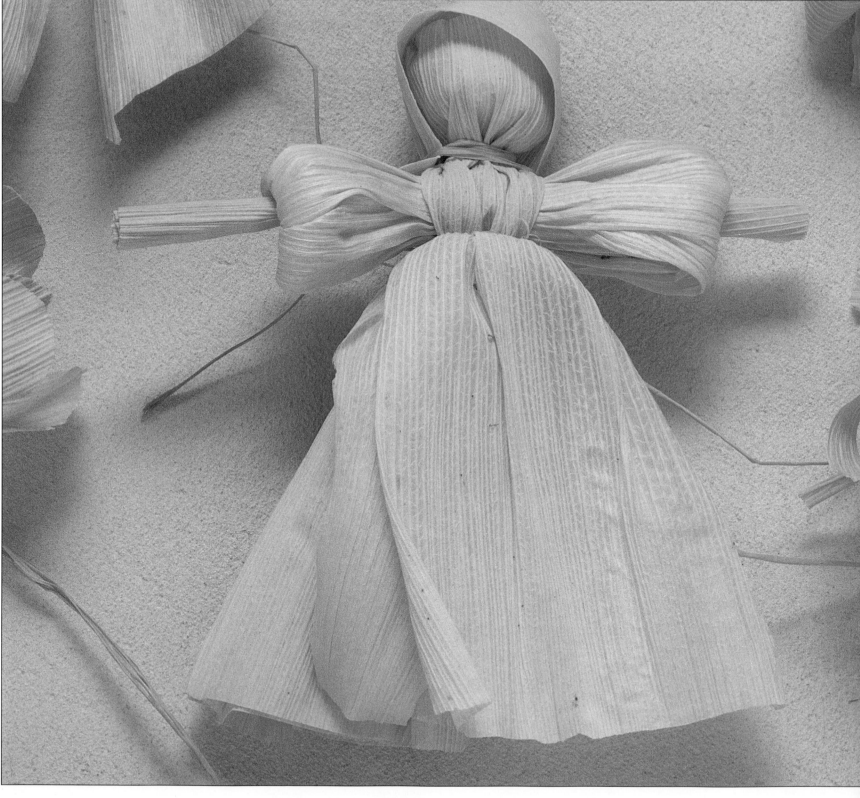

CORN-HUSK DOLLS

You don't have to live in the country and have a cornfield to make corn-husk dolls. Fresh corn on the cob from the grocery store will provide an ample supply of husks. Cut the stem end off the corn, close to the point where the kernels begin. Then slip the husks off, discarding the tough, coarse, dark green ones. Lay the soft inside ones on paper in a single layer to dry. When they are stiff and crisp, they are ready to be made into dolls.

Soak about twelve husks in a bowl of warm water for about ten minutes. Take out only as many as you need for each step, leaving the others in the water.

Stack five or six long husks with all the narrow ends at the top and tie them into a bundle, about two inches from the top.

As if you were rolling a sleeping bag, tightly roll the narrow ends down as far as the place where you tied them. Turn the husks so this is at the bottom and hold this roll between your left thumb and index finger.

Pretend you are peeling a banana and pull the husks one by one down over the rolled part, catching each under your left thumb as it is pulled down. Each one should be as smooth and tight as you can get it, and spread around the rolled husks from side to side. Tie the husks again, right under the lump formed by the rolled husks.

To make the arms, take three narrow husks (or split wider ones by pulling them apart lengthwise) and tie them together at one end. Braid these and tie at the other end. Or, you can take a wider husk and simply roll it into a long pencil shape and tie in the center to hold it.

Hold the armless doll facing you—the smoothest side of the head will be the face—and lift the two top husks away from the others. Push the rolled or braided arms right up against the tied neck under these two husks, and fold them back down over the arms. Tie just below these husks to form a waist.

Corn-husk dolls make attractive decorations for a kitchen.

Save the inner husks from ears of corn to make corn-husk dolls.

With another narrow husk, make a shawl over the doll's shoulders and bring the ends down, crossing them in front at the waist. Tie the waist again.

Take one perfect wide husk and lay it, wide side up, over the front of the doll, so that the widest end is over the face and the pointed end is about halfway down the skirt. Tie once more around the waist, securing this husk over the rest. Pull the husk down and smooth it over the skirt to make an apron.

Using scissors, trim the skirt evenly so the doll will stand, and trim the arms to a natural-looking length.

While the doll is still wet, you can shape the arms to hold something or turn them up or down. Tie them in the posi-tion you like. After the doll is completely dry (let it rest overnight, at least), cut these threads away and the arms will remain in place. You may have to trim the skirt again slightly after the husks are dry.

Cut the pointed end off a husk to make a square and place it over the doll's head for a bonnet. Fold it over in the back and tie in place until it dries. When the doll is dry, cut the threads and secure the hat with a drop of glue.

Corn-husk dolls traditionally had no faces, but there is no reason why you can't add your own personal touch and draw one. Be sure the doll is completely dry and use colored pencils to draw the face. Ink will spread, so don't use mark-ers or paints.

Hancock Shaker Village in Massachusetts is fortunate to have a craftsman who is an expert in box making.

STENCILED SHAKER SPICE SET

Round Shaker boxes make good storage containers in the kitchen, where their tight lids keep contents clean and dry and their flat tops make them easy and attractive to stack. Although they may be used plain, they are even more decorative if they are stenciled.

Choose any stencil pattern that fits your kitchen or make a simple design like the one pictured on the opposite page. Trace onto mylar stencil paper and cut carefully, using an X-acto knife and working on a sheet of glass. Trim any rough places so all the edges are smooth.

If your box is made of unfinished wood, cover the surface with a coat of clear sealer or a medium-toned stain. (Be careful of pine stains, since they often give a yellowish cast

to light wood. Cherry is a nice shade.) When the box has dried thoroughly, lightly buff with fine sandpaper to smooth the surface.

Decide where you will put your stencil, and mark the box lightly with a pencil to center a single design. If you are using a smaller motif repeated as a border, determine how far from the edge you want it and mark the stencil at that point so you can line the mark up with the edge each time and keep the border straight. Trace the outline of the box onto paper, cut it out, and fold it in pie-shaped wedges to get even measurements for placement.

Using a small stencil brush, put a tiny dab of stencil paint on the tops of the bristles and rub back and forth on a paper towel until no wet paint rubs off, and only dry color is left. Tape the stencil to the box. Working from the outer edge of each stencil opening to the center, rub the color from the brush, creating the pattern. To make color tones deeper, go over a section several times. Do not be tempted to hasten the process by applying more paint, since this will cause the paint to run under the edge of the stencil.

When the design is completed you can coat the box with a clear satin finish spray, sanding lightly between coats, or you can leave it as is. The finish coat will protect the stenciling if the boxes are washed.

Plain, unfinished surfaces of boxes and baskets are just right for decorating with simple stenciled designs.

© Robert Perron

COUNTRY COOKING

WOOD STOVES

A wood stove is the heart of a country kitchen—in fact, of the country home itself. On a frosty evening it is a gathering place; its warmth and the aromas from its oven seem to draw everyone closer to it and to each other. While some stoves are there just for appearances, if yours is in working order (and most are), it would be a shame not to cook and heat with it.

Using a wood stove is mostly a matter of common sense and a few principles of physics. If you remember that fire requires oxygen, smoke rises, and small wood burns faster, you will be able to build and maintain a good fire.

The dampers (the vents that allow air into stoves and chimneys) vary from stove to stove, but most have one beside the firebox (the chamber where the fire is), one on the back of the top above the oven, and one on the stovepipe near the wall. The trick is to adjust these so the fire gets enough air to burn without letting all the heat go up the chimney.

To start a fire, open all three dampers as far as possible. Put three or four sheets of crumpled newspaper into the firebox, then a few sticks of thin split kindling, then two larger pieces of wood, also split. Don't stack these solidly, but put them at enough of an angle so air can circulate between them. Light the paper with a match and close the door. The fire should be burning merrily in a few minutes, after which you can open the door and add some larger pieces of wood.

WOOD STOVE SAFETY

A wood stove in your home presents certain problems not associated with an electric range, and it is *essential* that you consider these before installing or using one. Brick, tile, stone, or other fire-resistant surfaces must be underneath the stove and extend out several inches on all sides. Failing this, an insulated metal "stove board" can be used to keep it off the floor. The stove should *never* sit on wood, linoleum, or carpet.

The stove should sit at least 24 inches from the wall unless the wall is made of brick or stone. The area where the stovepipe connects to the chimney must be fireproof; any portion of the stove or pipe should be at least 18 inches from an unprotected surface.

Since each state has its own regulations, it is best to call your local fire chief or contact your insurance company for a brochure with exact specifications.

Be sure to inspect the inside of your chimney and stovepipe regularly for creosote, which causes chimney fires. Have them cleaned whenever there is buildup. Always check chimneys before their first use in the fall to be sure they haven't become homes to nesting birds during the summer!

© Lynn Karlin

The many surfaces of a wood stove each have their uses for cooking, warming, drying, and setting bread to rise.

Never feed a fire through the top of the stove—it is dangerous and allows smoke to escape into the room. When the fire has caught well, close down the dampers, always starting with those at the bottom. You will soon learn how to regulate these to give you the heat you want. To prevent smoking, close the bottom damper and open the chimney damper a little more. For safety, the chimney damper should always be open when the bottom damper is open.

To cook on the stove, you move a pan and adjust the damper instead of turning a dial. The surface above the firebox is the hottest; over the oven is cooler.

Although not as useful as a cookstove, an old-fashioned pot-bellied stove provides warmth and cheer to a kitchen.

BAKING BREAD IN A WOOD STOVE

There is no scientific reason why bread should taste better baked in a wood stove, but everyone seems to agree that it does. Bread is also the easiest thing for a new wood-stove cook to try, since it is forgiving and can withstand irregular and uneven temperatures. It may get a little crusty or brown on one side, but it will still be delicious. As a showoff piece, nothing beats homemade loaves of bread fresh from the oven.

A little basic understanding of the wood-stove oven will be helpful before you start to bake. Check its heat with a thermometer and see if the dial on the door is correct. If it isn't, you need to know how far it is off and in which direction, or you will have to regularly use an inside thermometer. Be sure the oven damper is in the right position to let air circulate around it. The fire should be burning well ahead of baking time.

Hardwood is best for baking because it burns slowly and evenly, as well as hotter. It also makes a good bed of coals, which helps to keep the oven temperature even.

© E. Gebhardt/FPG International

Modern designs in wood stoves often make efficient heaters.

LIGHT WHEAT BREAD

¾ cup sugar

3 teaspoons salt

¼ cup vegetable oil

4 cups lukewarm milk

2 packages dry yeast, dissolved in ½ cup lukewarm water

4 cups whole-wheat flour

8 cups white flour

Combine sugar, salt, and oil with milk and add yeast. Stir in flour a cup at a time, beginning with the whole-wheat, then alternating between the two, until the dough is stiff. Turn dough out onto a well-floured board and knead for 15 minutes, adding remaining flour to the board as necessary.

Place in a large greased bowl, cover with a towel, and let rise on the warming shelf of your stove until doubled in bulk. Punch down with a floured fist and let rise again. Punch down, divide into fourths, and shape into loaves. Place these in greased pans and let rise again. Bake in a 350°F oven for 45 minutes or until the bread feels crisp and hollow when tapped with your finger. During the baking, move the loaves around twice to make sure they bake evenly. This recipe makes four loaves, but may be easily cut in half for two loaves.

INDIAN PUDDING

Few people are so extravagant in these days of rising energy costs as to bake a dessert for three hours in a gas or electric oven. But the wood-stove oven is warm whenever the stove is busy heating the kitchen, and requires only an occasional small log to maintain the temperature needed to bake Indian Pudding. No wonder it is a favorite!

3 cups milk

3 tablespoons yellow cornmeal

⅓ cup molasses

1 teaspoon ginger

¼ teaspoon cinnamon

¼ teaspoon salt

1 egg, beaten

1 tablespoon butter

1 cup cold milk

Heat the milk in a heavy saucepan and slowly stir in the cornmeal, molasses, spices, and salt. Continue stirring over low heat until the mixture begins to thicken, about 10 minutes. Remove from the heat and stir in the egg and butter. Pour into a heavy, well-greased baking dish. Bake at 300°F for about 30 minutes. Pour cold milk over the top, and do not stir. Bake, uncovered, at 250°F for 2 hours or until all the milk has been absorbed and the pudding is thick and dark. If the pudding seems to be scorching at the edges, add a little more milk. Serve hot with cream or a scoop of vanilla ice cream.

Makes 4 servings.

Crusty bread, fresh from the oven of your wood stove, is the delicious reward for the baker.

BRUNSWICK STEW

This Southern classic is perfect for slow simmering on the back of the wood stove or in a cast-iron kettle over an open fire, as it was originally made.

1 chicken (about 6 pounds), cut into pieces

2 tablespoons cooking oil

10 small onions, peeled

5 carrots, cut in chunks

Boiling water

Sprig of fresh thyme or ½ teaspoon dried

3 cups fresh or frozen lima beans

3 cups fresh or frozen corn

Salt (to taste)

Pepper (to taste)

Brown the chicken pieces in oil in a heavy skillet, then remove to cooking pot. Sauté the onions until light brown in the same skillet and add to the pot, along with the carrots. Cover with boiling water and add thyme. Simmer slowly until the meat is tender. Stir in beans and corn and cook until beans are done (if both vegetables are fresh, the beans will take longer than the corn, which is why you should use them as a test).

Makes 6 servings.

KITCHEN FIREPLACES

In early homes, the fireplace was not merely a place to cook, it was the center of the home's activity, especially in winter. It was the only source of heat and often light as well. Suspended strings of fruit dried over its mantel. Fireplaces were huge—the openings often tall enough to stand in—and with their ovens and hearths they took up an entire wall. In the winter, most of the household activities were carried out within the radius of its warmth.

Whatever the size of your fireplace, building a fire is much the same, as is its basic equipment. You will need andirons or a fireplace grate, the purpose of which is to support the wood and let air circulate from underneath. You should also have a fire screen to place over the opening while you are not actually using the fire. This is a simple but necessary safety precaution to keep flying sparks and falling logs contained. A pair of long-handled tongs and a poker are useful, too.

This fireplace in a Virginia restoration shows samples of early American implements.

© Mark E. Gibson

The fireplace is a central point for decorating as well as for family conversation.

Franklin stoves heat a room more efficiently than a fireplace.

To build a fire, be sure the damper is open and begin with a few sheets of tightly twisted newspaper. Lay these on the hearth between the andirons or underneath the grate. Over these lay several pieces of split kindling, then two or three small split logs. Light the newspaper. After the kindling is burning well and the larger pieces have caught, you may want to add a little more wood.

A small fire is all that is needed—a roaring bonfire is unsafe and sends too much heat up the chimney. Most cooking is done with hot coals, not the flame, so a cooking fire should be built well in advance and with good hardwood so a bed of coals will form in the fireplace.

FIREPLACE UTENSILS

Unique tools were created for use in and around the fireplace and some of these are still available to collectors. Because of renewed interest in fireplaces, Dutch ovens are being manufactured again, and S-hooks are still made by blacksmiths.

Harder to find are old ash peels—long-handled, flat, shovel-like implements used for scooping up and raking out ashes and hot coals. Shorter-handled wooden bread and pie peels were used to remove baked goods from brick ovens beside the fireplace.

Wafer irons were like waffle irons, but made flat wafers that could be rolled and filled with berries and fresh cream. They are rectangular with long tonglike handles. Also of cast-iron were toast racks that held bread above the coals for browning. Hanging pots with wire or perforated metal insert baskets that can be suspended over the pot by a hook on their bales are sometimes found. These were for straining and removing cooked vegetables steaming over a boiling pot.

Unusual pierced-tin drums on long wooden handles were for roasting precious coffee beans, and long-handled pans, much like bed-warming pans but with holes in the bottom, were for roasting chestnuts.

Perhaps the most interesting of all were the reflector ovens, half-round tin boxes that stood in front of the fire,

Fireplace and utensils at the Bonney House in Historic Bath, North Carolina.

caught its heat, and reflected it onto the meat or baking foods on the rack inside. Fancier models even had a little sliding door in the back so the cook could check the progress of the roast or baste it without lifting and turning the whole oven around to look in the front.

Pots, Dutch ovens, and frying pans are still being manufactured in cast-iron and can make an interesting collection in themselves if the antique examples are not available.

Fireplaces are often equipped with some built-in means of suspending a pot over the fire, either an iron rod set into the sides and running the width of the masonry or a crane that swings out on a hinge. Pots are suspended from these on S-hooks.

Soups, stews, and water for boiling can be hung from these hooks. The more likely the contents of the pot are to burn and stick in the pot, the farther they should be pushed to the side and away from the direct flame. Water can hang right over the flame as long as the pot doesn't boil dry.

The mainstay of fireplace cooking is the Dutch oven, a heavy cast-iron pot with a flat bottom and a lip around the edge that extends about a half-inch beyond the lid. Older Dutch ovens sometimes had rounded bottoms and three short legs that held them off the hearth and allowed the coals to be raked under them.

These ovens are used for baking biscuits, pies, and cakes as well as for roasting potatoes and meats (they're perfect for pot roast) or stews.

The oven is first heated by setting it over a layer of hot coals raked to one side of the hearth. The lid can be suspended by an S-hook over the fire to heat.

Biscuits, rolls, pies, or cakes are set inside the oven in round pans. Batter breads, such as corn bread, can be poured directly into the oven. After the lid is in place, hot coals are scooped onto the top of the oven, where the lip holds them in place. Fresh coals are raked underneath. Since the bottom of the pot is directly on the coals, these should not be as hot as the top layer.

To fry food in a fireplace, rake a layer of hot coals out onto the hearth and set the frying pan directly on top. Or, if you have a "spider," a little frame with short legs, you

An interpreter demonstrates various fireplace cooking implements at Tryon Place in North Carolina.

© Mark E. Gibson

A hearty stew can be cooked in a Dutch oven placed on the hearth or in a kettle hung over the fire.

can set that over the coals and cook with the frying pan on it. There are also cast-iron frying pans made with little feet attached for this purpose.

Broiling is the easiest method in terms of equipment, but it requires a good bed of coals without a high flame. Small meats such as sausages can be roasted on long forks held over the fire. Larger roasts and poultry are hung beside the fire or suspended over it on spits.

Potatoes can be roasted by burying them in hot ashes on the warm bricks where the fire has been burning. Corn, a fireplace favorite, can be stripped of its silks without removing the husks, soaked in cool water for about 10 minutes, then re-covered with the husks and placed directly on the hot coals to steam.

DUTCH-OVEN CORNPONE

1 cup flour

¾ cups stone-ground cornmeal

2 tablespoons sugar

½ teaspoon salt

1 tablespoon baking powder

1 cup buttermilk (or substitute ½ cup milk and ½ cup sour cream)

1 egg, beaten

2 tablespoons salad oil

Grease the entire inside of a Dutch oven with oil and preheat it and the lid by placing directly on the hot coals.

Sift the dry ingredients together. Add buttermilk, egg, and oil to the dry ingredients and mix well, but do not beat.

Sprinkle a little dry cornmeal inside the preheated oven, making sure to coat both the sides and bottom lightly, and pour the batter in. Replace the lid and cover with coals. Check it in about 15 minutes, at which time the cornpone should be done. If not, carefully replace the lid and coals and bake for another 5 minutes.

Makes 8 servings.

DUTCH-OVEN POT ROAST

A heavy, cast-iron Dutch oven set over the coals provides just the right combination of fast and slow cooking required for a tender, juicy pot roast.

4 pounds thick chuck or other roasting cut of beef

10 small onions, sliced

2 cups canned tomatoes and their juice

Salt (to taste)

Pepper (to taste)

Heat the Dutch oven over the coals until quite hot, add a little oil, and quickly sear the meat on all sides. Remove the meat and add the onions, stirring until slightly soft. Add the meat on top of the onions, then the tomatoes with their juice, and salt and pepper. Add whatever herbs you like and cover the oven. Place in the coals and rake a few coals over the top. The oven should not sit in a deep bed of very hot coals, since the meat needs to cook slowly. Check the meat after an hour and add more liquid if needed (you can use water, beef broth, or more tomato juice). As the meat cooks, the onions will help make it more tender. The roast is done when it is easily pierced with a sharp-tined cooking fork.

Makes 8 servings.

The kitchen at George Washington's home in Mount Vernon provides inspiration to modern decorators.

CHAPTER FOUR

USING YOUR COUNTRY KITCHEN

THE FRAGRANT KITCHEN

No potpourri can match or even imitate the warm and wonderful aromas that come from a busy kitchen. The fragrance of herbs growing on the windowsill, hot bread or spicy cookies in the oven, tinged with a hint of woodsmoke, are among the most memorable sensory delights that a country kitchen can offer.

But even without the potted herbs and the unmistakable note of a wood stove in the air, you can bring the country to your kitchen with a few well-chosen spices simmered on the back of your stove or placed in an open jar near the sink. The materials for a kitchen potpourri are right on the spice shelf.

For a blend to simmer, choose hard, sturdy spices. Mix any combination of whole allspice, cloves, coriander, cardamom, cracked nutmeg, broken cinnamon sticks, and pieces of gingerroot. Add bits of dried orange and lemon peel. This same mixture can be reused often and revitalized periodically with a handful of fresh spices. To package this blend as a gift, put it in a glass-topped canning jar or an apothecary jar with an instruction tag that says to add a quarter-cup of spices to a quart of water and simmer slowly on the stove.

Dried herbs can be added to this blend or mixed without the spices for a potpourri as fresh as a spring breeze blowing in the open window. Whole bay leaves, lemon verbena, sprigs of thyme and savory, bee balm, marjoram, oregano, or basil can be mixed with spices or used alone. Or make bouquets of fresh rosemary and any or all of the herbs above and put them in a vase on the kitchen table. Here they are as useful to the cook as they are fragrant.

SETTING A TABLE.

Fortunate indeed are those whose kitchen is large enough to allow for the traditional family table. The very center of household activity, the table can nevertheless be set for dinner with all the grace of a dining room. Pottery plates in spatter or redware, curved flatware based on old pewter patterns, or wooden-handled utensils set on a homespun tablecloth make a gracious table setting, rich in country tradition. A wooden or crockery bowl or toleware dish of fruit would be a good centerpiece, or in the fall, an arrangement of dried grasses in a tin coffeepot. Candles for this setting could be placed in old tin "hog scraper" push-up candlesticks; the candles themselves could be bayberry.

Use stenciled napkins of unbleached muslin, too informal for the dining room but just the right touch for a dinner in the kitchen. Or use brightly colored napkins in a variety of colors. Use unmatched plates and different settings, but with coordinating napkins for each.

For a Victorian family touch, use silver napkin rings, again unmatched and this time historically accurate as well. Napkin rings were given as gifts or "presentations" and were usually unmatched or engraved with names so each person could return his napkin, neatly rolled, to the proper ring for future use.

For a Western touch, use bandannas for napkins, pulling these from the center into napkin rings. Country table settings shouldn't be stodgy, and unusual additions can add a touch of surprise to table accessories and decorations.

TINY WREATHS FOR NAPKIN RINGS

Small vines are usually quite supple and easy to work with, especially when freshly cut. Wrap the vines around a small bottle to shape them in perfect circles, slipping them off and intertwining the ends to hold the wreath in shape. These informal napkin rings can be used plain or decorated with dried flowers. A red bow will give a Christmas touch, and a gold ribbon is appropriate for harvest dinners.

Bake tiny braided bread wreaths (see page 108), but instead of laying them flat to bake, wrap them around tin cannoli forms or empty tomato-paste cans. The weight of the wreath will flatten the bottom side as it bakes, but the rest of the wreath will hold its shape. Bake them only until they are brown and be sure the mold or can is greased well so the finished wreath will slide off easily.

© Robert Perron

Kitchen table settings can be as offbeat and creative as the materials at hand.

A kitchen setting lends a homey atmosphere to family meals.

Fancy-shaped candles such as these are made in molds, not by dipping.

MAKING YOUR OWN CANDLES

Even though candles are no longer a necessity, they are welcome for their soft, warm light. In a kitchen, their glow is reminiscent of firelight.

To make candles, use candle wax, not paraffin, which has a lower melting point and will not burn properly. Likewise, use woven wicking; do not substitute wrapping string. Both wax and wick are available at craft stores.

You will need a container as deep as the length of the candle (such as a large juice can). Set the can of wax inside a kettle of boiling water and heat it to 165 to 170° F. Wax that is too cool will thicken and make dipping difficult, while wax that is too hot will melt off the previously dipped layer. Once the wax is hot enough, you can remove the pan from the stove and work until the wax cools.

Cut a wick twice the length you want your candles to be plus 3 inches. Tie the wick around a stick, looping it in two half-hitches so the wicks hang down about 2 inches apart. Dip both wicks into the wax, lift them out, and let the excess wax drip back into the container until the candles are cool enough to touch. Pull each wick straight after the initial dipping. After that, the candle will keep its shape without pulling. Continue dipping, letting the wax cool a little between dips, until the candles are the desired thickness.

You will soon learn just how long to leave the candle in the hot wax each time. If you leave it too long, the heat will melt the previous coat and the candle will get smaller instead of larger. If you are making thin tapers, be sure they are sturdy enough to stand firmly.

Allow the finished candles to harden overnight before trimming their bases with a sharp knife. Leave them in pairs until they're used and hang them on pegs or hooks.

If you have a lot of old candle ends, you can reuse the wax to make new candles. Before melting, sort the candle stubs by color and combine only those that are compatible. Blues and greens can be mixed, as can reds and yellows. Do not combine red and green or you will get a dull brown color. White candles can be mixed with any color.

The warm glow of candlelight softens and warms any area.

STOCKING THE PANTRY

Filling the pantry or jelly cupboard with neat and glistening jars full of the fruits of the harvest is not a tradition reserved only for those who live in the country. Farm housewives aren't the only ones who can turn out beautiful jellies, preserves, chutneys, and pickles. The tiniest backyard garden can produce fruits and vegetables for preserving, and those without a backyard have an abundance of produce as close as the nearest farmers' market.

There are very few tricks to fine preserving, but a few safety precautions are essential. Be sure that all your jars and utensils are clean and sterilized. Boil the lids and jars for ten minutes just before filling them. Process sealed jars for fifteen minutes in boiling water to ensure a perfect seal. Although most older recipes do not say to do this, modern research has proven it to be necessary. You should add this step to all recipes. Paraffin seals are not safe; all products should be put in jars with rubber-lined lids.

The modern, French canning jars make excellent sealed storage for kitchen or pantry shelves.

Be sure to follow the safety rules for canning and preserving, using metal lids and processing for a tight seal.

The only other general rule is to use fresh, perfect produce. Jam is not the place for old, bruised fruit or berries. Cucumbers for pickles should be very fresh and firm.

In pickling, vegetables are cut or sliced, sometimes soaked in ice or salt water, and cooked briefly in a brine made of vinegar, sugar, and spices. The vegetables are removed, packed into hot jars, and the brine poured over them. The sealed jars are then processed in boiling water to seal. Follow the same procedure for relishes, but use finely cut or ground vegetables instead of large chunks.

While glass-lidded jars are attractive, they provide no means for testing the seal for safety in storage.

© A.G.E. Fotostock/FPG International

The bounty of a garden or farm market can be preserved in jams,
jellies, pickles, conserves, butters, and vinegars.

For preserves and jams, fruit is combined with sugar, then boiled until a small amount of the hot mixture slides from a large spoon in a sheet instead of separate drops. Use whole or large-cut fruit for preserves, and use crushed fruit for jam.

Jelly is made by cooking the clear juice strained from cooked fruit and boiling it until it reaches the jelly stage, as above. Some fruits, such as peaches, which lack pectin, can be made into jelly by adding pectin-rich fruit or by using a commercial pectin. Each of these products is used differently, so always follow the directions that are enclosed in the pectin package.

Conserves and chutneys are similar to jams, but have added ingredients such as nuts and raisins. Use vinegar and less sugar than jam for chutney, which is used as a condiment with meats and main dishes. Fruit butters are made from pureed fruit, which is cooked very slowly until it is dark and thick.

Old glass canning jars should be used only for brined pickles or those products that will be stored in the refrigerator.

© F. Stein/FPG International

'BREAD AND BUTTER' PICKLES

*2 quarts cucumbers, thinly
    sliced*

2 medium onions, sliced

1 garlic clove, thinly sliced

¼ cup salt

1¼ cups cider vinegar

1½ cups sugar

½ teaspoon turmeric

½ teaspoon celery seed

1 tablespoon mustard seed

½ cup water

Combine the cucumbers, onions, garlic, and salt in a large pot and cover with crushed ice. Stir occasionally for 3 hours. Drain and rinse well. Combine the vinegar, sugar, and spices, bring to a boil, and boil for 5 minutes. Add the water if there is not enough juice to cover the vegetables. Pour the pickles into hot, sterilized jars, seal, and process 15 minutes in boiling water.

Makes 4 pints.

CRABAPPLE JELLY

Cut crabapples in half and simmer in water to barely cover. When the crabapples are soft, mash and continue cooking for 5 minutes. Pour into a jelly bag and allow to drip overnight. Do not squeeze. Measure the juice and combine with an equal amount of sugar. Boil to the jelly point, which will probably take only a few minutes unless the apples have been stored for a long time. Skim froth from top and ladle into hot, sterilized jars. Seal and process for 15 minutes in boiling water.

PEAR CHUTNEY

5 pounds pears (Bosc or Anjou)

½ pound raisins

2 large onions, chopped

1 lemon, thinly sliced

2 cups vinegar

3 cups sugar

½ cup fresh lemon or lime juice

¼ cup fresh ginger, sliced

Peel, core, and chop the pears. Combine the remaining ingredients and cook until thick, stirring often. Seal in hot, sterilized jars and process 15 minutes in boiling water.

Makes 3 pints.

For gifts of country preserves, cover the lids with circles of gingham or calico fabric.

© Hanson Carroll

Instead of hiding your preserves in a pantry, display them on open shelves.

Red chili peppers make a bright decoration while they remain handy for kitchen use.

© Robert Perron

PICKLED CHERRY PEPPERS

Red cherry peppers

Cider vinegar

Wash peppers well and pierce in several places with the tip of a knife. Pack the peppers as snugly as possible in hot, sterilized jars. Bring the vinegar to a boil and add to the jars. Seal and process 15 minutes in boiling water. To use in recipes calling for fresh peppers, simply rinse in cold water first.

PICCALILLI

6 green tomatoes

4 green bell peppers

2 sweet red peppers

1 hot pepper

5 onions

¼ cup salt

2½ cups brown sugar

1 teaspoon celery seed

1 tablespoon mustard seed

1 teaspoon whole cloves

1 tablespoon whole allspice

1¾ cups cider vinegar

Slice all the vegetables very thinly, toss with the salt, and let rest overnight. Rinse in cold water and drain well. Combine in a large pot with the other ingredients, bring to a boil, and simmer 15 minutes. Seal in hot, sterilized jars and process 15 minutes in boiling water.

Makes 3 pints.

© Hanson Carroll

A wood stove is the perfect place for slow simmering of fruit butters.

ONION BRAIDS, PEPPER STRINGS, AND SCHNITZ

In a Mediterranean country kitchen, long braids of onions, shallots, and garlic, and strings of bright red peppers decorate the walls and serve as handy ingredients for the cook. Strings of hot peppers are also a familiar sight in the Southwest. Strings of drying apples are a common sight in Pennsylvania Dutch farmhouses, while ears of popcorn or grinding corn on an iron "drying tree" can be seen in homes from New England to the Southwest.

The purpose in hanging onions and garlic is not to dry but to store them in an airy place where they will keep well and be handy for use. Hot peppers, corn, and apples are left hanging only until completely dry, then may be stored in containers.

Garlic is best preserved in an open, airy place, such as a string kept handy in the kitchen.

© Hogben/FPG International

To make braids or strings, use onions, garlic, or shallots with their tops still attached. When these tops are dry but not brittle, tie six of them together and begin braiding. Add more onions as there is room. When the string is long enough, tie the braid and cut off the remaining ends.

Hot peppers, such as chilies or the long, red, Italian variety, can be strung on long threads to dry, or you can braid jute cord tightly, slipping pepper stems into the braid as you work.

SCHNITZ UN KNEPP

2 cups dried apples

3 pounds ham hocks

1 egg

¼ cup milk

2 tablespoons butter

2 cups flour

3 teaspoons baking powder

¼ teaspoon salt

Soak the dried apples in water to cover overnight. The next day scrub and dry the ham hocks and simmer in water for about 3 hours. Add the apples and soaking water. Boil together for 45 minutes to make the knepp.

Beat the egg and add milk and butter. Sift and add the dry ingredients. Mix well, but don't overbeat. Drop by spoonfuls into the boiling knepp. Cover tightly and steam for 15 minutes without raising the lid. Serve at once.

Makes 4 servings.

Strings of peppers and garlic, once they are dried, should be hung in a shady place.

Popcorn can be dried on the ears and hung as decoration.

Popcorn, seed corn, or varieties that will be ground for meal may also be braided by their husks or tied into bundles for drying. Corn is especially attractive displayed on a wrought-iron "drying tree," which holds the corn ears separately and hangs from a rafter or flat against a wall.

To dry apples, peel, core, and slice firm apples into thin rings and drop them into a bowl of water with a few drops of lemon juice. Remove the apples within ten minutes and pat dry. Thread these on a long string and hang in a clean, airy place, separating the rings. They are dry when they become leathery, and should then be stored in a tightly closed jar. Dried apples make excellent pies, but the favorite Pennsylvania Dutch use is in Schnitz un Knepp. (See recipe on page 93.)

© A. Giampiccolo/FPG International

Some fruits, such as apples, can be dried easily in the kitchen, while others require more complicated processing.

SHARING AND ENTERTAINING

A YANKEE BEAN SUPPER

In New England, a bean supper is more than just a meal. It is a social occasion and a major source of revenue for churches, fire departments, and a variety of other organizations.

But bean suppers don't have to be community events. As a way to entertain a group of friends informally in your own kitchen, the bean supper is perfect. The cooking is comparatively easy and nearly everything can be done ahead of time. A supper can be cooked by a single hostess or a group of friends working together. Individual guests can bring food, already prepared, or friends can gather to cut the slaw and make the corn bread as a group. But one person easily can give a bean supper alone.

The corn bread (or corn sticks, which will not dry out or crumble) can be baked a day or two early and stored in large plastic bags. The bread is better if it is reheated, covered with foil, shortly before serving. You can pile it in a large pan and put it in the oven when you take out the beans. This will warm and also crisp it.

The coleslaw can be cut and refrigerated for assembling on the day of the supper. The ham can be arranged on its platters in advance and refrigerated if it is to be served cold for the supper.

Although it is a bit more work, it is better to buy and bake hams instead of serving the canned versions. The hams can be cooked, cooled, and then sliced for serving cold or for rewarming on the griddle before serving. If your oven is big enough or the group a fairly small one, you can even bake a ham at the same time as the beans and serve it whole, letting guests do their own carving.

If you are using home-cooked ham and want to serve it cold, you can pre-slice it quite easily. Bone it while it is still warm, tie it firmly, and chill it. Then you can slice it with a sharp carving knife.

Everyone has a favorite recipe for baked beans and you will probably want to use your own. If you have them, soldier beans bake beautifully, but navy beans are more readily available. The following recipe will serve about twenty-five people and you can bake it in a large pan.

The oven of a wood stove is more economical for the long hours required to bake beans than a modern kitchen range.

Red kidney, soldier, Jacob's cattle, navy, pea, yellow-eye, and several other bean varieties work well for baking.

BAKED BEANS

8 cups dry soldier or navy beans

8 small onions (scored with a cross on the bottom)

1 pound salt pork, cut in 1-inch cubes

1 cup brown sugar

⅓ cup molasses

2 tablespoons salt

2 tablespoons dry mustard

1 tablespoon powdered ginger

1 tablespoon thyme

Cover the beans with cold water, bring to a boil, and boil for 2 minutes. Cover the pot, remove from the heat, and let stand 1 hour. Return to heat and slowly bring to a boil. Reduce the heat and simmer about an hour, or until the skins wrinkle and peel away when you blow on a few beans.

Drain (saving the liquid) and put the beans in a large baking pan with the remaining ingredients. Mix the ingredients among the beans evenly, then add the bean liquid to cover. Bake at 300°F for about 8 hours. Check every hour to make sure that the liquid isn't boiling away, and add more of the reserved liquid or hot water if needed. The beans can stay in the oven until you serve them, as long as you check the liquid level. Toward the end of baking, let the liquid level drop a little so the beans will not be too juicy.

No matter how many corn sticks you make, there will not be any left over. Plan to serve at least two apiece. Some people won't take two, but many will take five! The best way to prepare a lot of them is to line up all of the ingredients in order of use and keep several batches going at once. Since cast-iron corn-stick pans should be used hot, this "assembly line" method saves heating the pans each time. Brush the crumbs out with a stiff natural bristle brush and apply a fresh coat of oil with a paper towel before pouring in the next batch of batter. If you can't get cornstick pans, this same recipe can be used to make corn muffins.

By mixing the ingredients for one batch as you bake the previous one, the whole process takes surprisingly little time. You can keep three batches going at once with a little practice. Each batch makes a dozen.

CORN STICKS

1 cup yellow cornmeal

1 cup flour

2 tablespoons sugar

¾ teaspoon salt

1 tablespoon baking powder

1 cup sour milk (sweet will do)

1 egg, beaten

2 tablespoons melted butter

½ teaspoon crumbled rosemary or sage

Sift the dry ingredients together, then add the remaining ingredients to the bowl. Mix well and pour into greased muffin tins. Bake for 20 minutes at 425°F, check, and continue baking until they are golden but not dry.

For coleslaw, shred a large head of cabbage for each dozen people. Once shredded, it can be stored in the refrigerator in plastic bags. Make the dressing in a large jar and refrigerate. Mix 2 cups of dressing to 6 cups of shredded cabbage, and let stand at room temperature for 3 hours before serving.

COLESLAW DRESSING

4 cups sour cream

1 teaspoon dry mustard

1 teaspoon black pepper

¾ cup sugar

1 cup cider vinegar

1 teaspoon celery seed

2 teaspoons salt

Put ingredients in a jar and shake to blend.

For dessert, you can ask guests to bring their favorite pie. Serve it either plain or with vanilla ice cream. Another possible dessert, which can be prepared in advance and placed into the oven just as you sit down to eat, is baked apples. Stand them in rows in cake pans to bake, and serve them hot with fresh cream poured on top.

As a variation, leave out the maple syrup, use 1½ cups of sugar, and add a cup of fresh whole cranberries to the nuts and currants. You will have to pile this mixture on top of the apples and possibly sprinkle the leftover berries around the pan between the apples.

MAPLE BAKED APPLES

12 firm, tart apples

½ cup chopped walnuts

½ cup dried currants

½ cup sugar

1 teaspoon cinnamon

Pinch of nutmeg

¼ cup maple syrup

Core the whole apples, but do not peel. Stand them in baking pans. Mix the nuts, currants, sugar, and spices and spoon a little into the cavity of each apple. Spoon just a little maple syrup over each apple and bake in a 350°F oven for 30 to 45 minutes, or until the apples are soft. Carefully remove the apples with a large spoon and serve hot, with a spoonful of the syrup that has accumulated in the bottom of the baking pan poured over each apple. Pass a pitcher of cream.

© Jerry W. Myers/FPG International

Firm apples are best for baking whole, but nearly any tart apple works well.

Nearly every room in the house, including the living room, allows for creative Christmas decorating.

© Hanson Carroll

HOME TO THE CHRISTMAS KITCHEN

In a country home, the kitchen is always the busiest place, but at Christmas it seems as though everything is happening there at once. Children are making gifts for their grandmother at the kitchen table, the counters are spread with racks of cookies to be packed into gift boxes, and the top of the stove has full cookie sheets waiting for space in the oven. A bowl of apples and a jar of whole cloves sit handy in case anyone has a spare moment to turn them into fragrant pomanders, and a string of apple slices is drying over the wood stove.

With all this activity, there is hardly any need to think about how to decorate the kitchen for the holidays. The very busyness of the season decorates it for you! Let the kitchen be your workshop (and Santa's) by standing rolls of bright-colored gift wrap in a basket, along with tape, scissors, tags, and ribbons, ready for anyone who needs to wrap a present. Create a seasonal tablecloth from a length of calico in a Christmas print—you don't even have to hem the ends if you cut them neatly. Use red or green napkins and put a few extra Christmas tree ornaments in a wooden salad bowl as a centerpiece. Tuck a few sprigs of greens between the ornaments or mix in large pinecones.

Make a quick arrangement of evergreen tips and spice it up with a few dried red peppers on florists' wire. If you have access to bright red berries such as bittersweet, add a few sprigs to the peppers and greens. Be careful, however, to keep any fresh evergreens—arrangements, roping, swags, or wreaths—away from the stove or fireplace.

DECORATING EVERGREEN WREATHS

While a plain evergreen wreath is at home anywhere (except near a stove or fireplace), there are certain ornaments that make a wreath particularly suitable for a kitchen. Tie bows of narrow red satin ribbon around pretzels and hang on the wreath. Attach red-and-white-striped peppermint candies to florists' picks and stud the center of the wreath. Or use candy canes. Small gingerbread people with pieces of maraschino cherries for their faces will dress up a wreath, as will small sugar cookies in traditional holiday shapes. Decorate these with colored sugar or more elaborately with frosting.

A simple evergreen wreath is a symbol of hospitality.

© Robert Perron

© Robert Perron

Wreaths of herbs and dried flowers will last all year.

Colored marzipan fruit will give a Della Robbia look to your wreath, but they are very likely to disappear, one by one, before Christmas Eve! To attach these or other soft items to the wreath, push florists' picks into their backs.

Decorate larger wreaths with an assortment of tin cookie cutters in holiday or other shapes, or use a combination of other old kitchen utensils from your collection. Bright dried red peppers are a good contrast to the deep green branches, as are fresh kumquats. Tie cinnamon sticks to the wreath with narrow red ribbon. Combine tiny wire whisks with miniature wooden spoons (both available at kitchen supply shops), tying them together in a cross with red ribbon and hanging on the wreath. Even a quick look around your kitchen will suggest other ornaments. These wreaths can be hung on the door or wall, or used as a centerpiece for the kitchen table.

Add decorations of bright fresh fruit to your holiday wreaths.

A WILLIAMSBURG WREATH
OF FRESH FRUIT

A welcoming circle of glossy broad-leaved evergreens and shining fresh fruit is a Southern tradition perfect for the kitchen door. If the weather is too severe to use fresh fruit outdoors, hang this wreath on a protected porch or use it indoors, replacing the fruit as necessary.

The base is a doughnut-shape, cut from plywood. It can be any size, but the ring itself should be at least 3 inches wide. (If the outer diameter is 12 inches, then the inner cutout diameter would be 6 inches.) Paint this base dark green and let it dry thoroughly. Stud the center with 2-inch nails, pounded all the way through so the surface has a row of pointed nails on one side, but is perfectly flat on the other. Wrap a loop of florists' wire around the frame for a hanger.

Impale bright red or green apples, oranges, lemons, limes, crabapples, or other bright fruit on the nails. These can be a mixture, balanced for size and color, or they can be a simple row of matching apples or crabapples. Cover the rest of the frame by tucking magnolia leaves and sprigs of boxwood or other greens between the fruit. You may have to wire or glue some of these in place if their stems will not hold securely under the fruit.

A WREATH OF DRIED APPLES

A circle of dried apple slices, their red peels left intact, is attractive in the kitchen at any time of year. Slice apples about a quarter-inch thick and dry as described on page 95. Or, if you have a wood stove, place the circles of apple on wire racks and dry in a slightly warm oven (leaving the door open) for several hours until they are leathery.

For the wreath, choose only the perfect center slices of uniform size and shape. Glue these in an overlapping row to a single crinkle-wire wreath ring. A glue gun will work best for this, since the glue dries quickly and remains pliable enough to secure the leathery apples. This simple wreath does not need a bow.

The pineapple is a traditional symbol of hospitality, popular in Williamsburg-style decorations.

Magnolia leaves and fresh fruit are hallmarks of the Williamsburg wreath.

A BREAD WREATH

What better way to welcome your friends to your country kitchen than with a decoration that combines two ancient symbols of hospitality—bread and the wreath. Mix half a batch of the bread recipe on page 66, substituting white flour for the whole wheat. Let it rise once as directed, then divide it into three equal parts. Let the dough rest for 10 minutes and knead it to remove as much air as possible.

Roll each of the three sections into a long rope. On a well-greased baking sheet, braid the three ropes of dough, forming them into a circle. Tuck the ends into the braid so it forms a continuous pattern. (If you cannot get a perfect join, don't worry. You can always cover it with a bow of red-and-white gingham.)

Brush the entire surface with lightly beaten egg white and let rest 10 minutes. Carefully brush the wreath with egg white again and bake in a 350°F oven for 45 minutes or until it is golden brown. Remove to a wire rack to cool.

You can either use this as an edible centerpiece on your table or hang it on the wall as a decoration. It will keep well outdoors as long as it is kept inside the storm door and out of the rain. When you are through with the wreath, hang it outdoors for the birds to enjoy.

Fresh breads, especially in wreath shapes, add to holiday decorations.

Let your festive foods decorate the kitchen at Christmas time.

KITCHEN METRICS

For cooking and baking convenience, use the following metric measurements:

SPOONS:

1/4 teaspoon = 1 milliliter
1/2 teaspoon = 2 milliliters
1 teaspoon = 5 milliliters
1 tablespoon = 15 milliliters
2 tablespoons = 25 milliliters
3 tablespoons = 50 milliliters

CUPS:

1/4 cup = 50 milliliters
1/3 cup = 75 milliliters
1/2 cup = 125 milliliters
2/3 cup = 150 milliliters
3/4 cup = 175 milliliters
1 cup = 250 milliliters

OVEN TEMPERATURES:

200° F = 100° C
225° F = 110° C
250° F = 120° C
275° F = 140° C
300° F = 150° C
325° F = 160° C
350° F = 180° C
375° F = 190° C
400° F = 200° C
425° F = 220° C
450° F = 230° C
475° F = 240° C

WEIGHT AND MEASURE EQUIVALENTS

1 inch = 2.54 centimeters
1 square inch = 6.45 square centimeters
1 foot = .3048 meters
1 square foot = 929.03 square centimeters
1 yard = .9144 meters
1 square yard = .84 square meters
1 ounce = 28.35 grams
1 pound = 453.59 grams

INDEX

A

American style, 13
Antiques, 50–52
Apples, dried, 91–5, 107
maple baked, 101
Architectural features, adding, 21
Auctions, 51

B

Baking in a woodstove, 65
Baskets, 49
Beams, 26, 28
Beans, baked, 99
Bean supper, 97
Boxes, 49
Braids, onion and garlic, 91–3
Bread baking, 65
corn, 97
light wheat, 66
wreath, 108
Brunswick stew, 67

C

Candles, 80
Canning jars, 17
Ceiling cornices, 28
Chair rails, 24, 26–7
Christmas decorations, 103
Chutney, 88
Coleslaw, 97, 100
Collecting utensils, 17, 50
Collections, displaying, 49
Colors, 18
Containers, 49
Cookbooks, old, 14
Cooking, 63
Cornbread, 97
sticks, 97, 100
Cornhusk dolls, 56
Cornpone, 74
Crabapple jelly, 88
Crafts, buying, 53

Crafts, wooden, 49
Curtains, 30

D

Displaying collections, 49
Dolls, cornhusk, 56
Dutch oven, 72
cornpone, 74
potroast, 74

E

Entertaining, 97
Evergreen wreaths, 104

F

Fireplace, 68
utensils, 71
Fire safety, woodstove, 64
Floorcloths, painted, 36, 40
Floor coverings, 18
Floors, 36–39
French Canadian style, 10
Fruit wreath, 106

G

Garlic braid, 92–3

H

Hooked rug making, 42
Hoosier cupboard, 10, 13

I

Indian pudding, 67

J

Jams, 86
Jellies, 82, 86, 88

L

Linens, 30, 78

M

Maple baked apples, 101
Marzipan, 105
Mediterranean style, 10
Moldings, decorative, 26

N

Napkin rings, 54, 78
Napkins, 30

O

Onion braids, 92–3

P

Panels, raised, 28
tin, 14, 45–47
Pantry, 82
Pear chutney, 88
Peppers, dried, 92
pickled, 91
Piccalilli, 91
Pickles, 82, 84, 87, 91
Pierced tin, 14, 45–47
Pie safe, 14, 45–47
Popcorn, 95
Potpourri, 77
Potroast, 74
Pottery, 78
Preserves, 82, 86
Pudding, Indian, 67

R

Rosemaling, 10
Rugs, 10, 18, 42
hooking, 42

S

Santa Fe style, 9
Scandinavian style, 10
Schnitz (dried apples), 91, 93
Shaker boxes, 60
Shallot braids, 92–3
Silver napkin rings, 54